# CHILDREN
## OF THE WORLD

### DR. DIANA PRINCE

*AuthorHouse™*
*1663 Liberty Drive*
*Bloomington, IN 47403*
*www.authorhouse.com*
*Phone: 1 (800) 839-8640*

*Published by AuthorHouse 03/22/2019*

*ISBN: 978-1-7283-0528-8 (sc)*
*ISBN: 978-1-7283-0529-5 (hc)*
*ISBN: 978-1-7283-0527-1 (e)*

*Library of Congress Control Number: 2019903441*

*Print information available on the last page.*

*Any people depicted in stock imagery provided by Getty Images are models, and such images are being used for illustrative purposes only.*
*Cover and photos on pages 3, 5, 7, 9, 11, 13, 17, 21, 25, 27, 29, 31, 33, and 37 are used with permission of Getty Images.*

*Author Photos:*
*Photos on pages 15, 19, 23, 35 and 39 are property of the Author.*

*This book is printed on acid-free paper.*

authorHOUSE®

# Contents

# List of Photos

# Foreword

*This book reveals how children, in different parts of the world, interact within their unique environments and cultures. It looks at both anthropology and geography through pictures that even the youngest child can relate to and understand.*

*It is designed to inform young readers and broaden their understanding of the values we all share as human beings. Most of all, it helps them to learn about this fascinating world around us.*

*This book is dedicated to the children of the world, who are our future. May they become the architects of peace in this world we share.*

# France

France is a country in Europe. The young girl in the picture lives in a small French village. She is carrying long loaves of bread called baguettes. This country is known throughout the world for its bread and cheeses. In the countryside, large vineyards also produce grapes for wine.

France had an important impact on world history. It was originally settled by Celtic tribes called the Gauls. Rome conquered it in the first century, and it was part of the Roman Empire for almost 400 years. The name "France" came from the Franks who claimed the area in the fifth century. They established a kingdom which lasted for several centuries until the French Revolution overturned the monarchy. The French Republic was established four years later in the year 1792.

Today there are more tourists visiting France than any other country. In Paris, the capital and largest city of France, there are world famous landmarks such as the Eiffel Tower, the cathedral called Notre Dame, and the Arc de Triumph.

At Versailles there is a famous palace with royal gardens. The Louvre Museum has some of the world's most famous art. The town of Carcassonne is famous for its stone fortress and medieval castle. At Arles there is a large amphitheater that was built by the Romans in the first century. The French Riviera is known for its beautiful beaches at Cannes, Nice and Saint-Tropez.

# Morocco

This young girl lives in Taroudant near the old town called the Medina. She sometimes helps her family take care of the goats and other animals that belong to the family. She also helps her mother with cooking.

Morocco, located in North Africa, is a land of both mountains and desert. Both Arabic and French are spoken here. Officially called the Kingdom of Morocco, it has both a king and a parliament. Morocco has a population of 34 million people.

Morocco has coastlines on both the Mediterranean Sea and the Atlantic Ocean. At one point there is only an eight-mile distance between Europe and Africa. This is the narrow passage of water called the Strait of Gibraltar. It separates Spain in the north from Morocco in the south.

On the north side, in Spain, is the Rock of Gibraltar which points skyward out of the water. On the Moroccan side is the mountain called Jebel Musa. Together they are what the ancients once called "the Pillars of Hercules". To the ancient Greeks, these two landmarks were considered the end of the earth, and boats were warned never to go beyond that point.

There is an interesting city in Morocco called Marrakesh. In the medina square, there is an interesting combination of shops, cafes, fortunetellers, fire eaters and snake charmers. It is like stepping back in time to a forgotten and magical world.

# New Zealand

The young girl in the picture is at a cultural festival celebrating the ancient traditions which her ancestors have honored for hundreds of years. She belongs to a tribe called the Maori. This celebration is held at a place called Ruatahune near Gisborne on the North Island of New Zealand.

The ancestors of this tribe came to New Zealand by boat from Polynesia over a thousand years ago. The Maoris call New Zealand "Aotearoa" which means "the land of the long white cloud." New Zealand is a country located in the Pacific Ocean, and it consists of two main islands.

On the North Island, there are active volcanoes. The most recent volcanic activity was in 2007 when Ruapehu erupted. There are five other volcanoes which are "dormant", which means that they have had no recent eruptions. The largest lake in New Zealand is Lake Taupo which lies in the center of a huge volcanic crater called a caldera.

South Island is the largest of the two islands. Here there are tall mountains called "the Southern Alps", with soaring mountain peaks. The tallest is Mount Cook which is over 12,000 feet high. During the Ice Age, huge glaciers carved steep rock formations and passageways into this region. Today, four million people live in New Zealand. The main language is English. Adventurers come here to observe rare and interesting animals, to watch whales, to ride kayaks and to explore caves.

# Austria

This young girl's family lives in a quiet mountain village in Austria. They own a small farm which provides milk and eggs for the family. They also have a small vegetable garden.

Austria, known for its spectacular mountain peaks and blue lakes, is one of the most beautiful places in the world. The highest altitude is over 12,000 feet. The people are healthy and active, and skiing and hiking are very popular.

From almost three million years ago up until the most recent ice age, glaciers passed through here scraping and gouging out many lakes in the alpine regions. The two largest are the Neusiedler Lake and Lake Constance. Some animals who make their homes here are falcons, swans, eagles and brown bears.

Located in Central Europe, Austria is a country with over nine million people. There are large cities with elaborate architecture, beautiful tree-lined parks and elegant castles. The main language is German. The capital is the city of Vienna, located on the Danube River. For 300 years it has been the home of the training school for the famous white Lipizzaner stallions and their skilled riders.

This region was once part of the Holy Roman Empire. Later, the Hapsburgs ruled for many centuries until 1918, and through marriages became one of the most powerful dynasties in history. Some of the world's most famous music composers, including Strauss, Mozart and Liszt, have come from Austria.

# Peru

This little girl lives in a place called Cuzco in Peru. She is part of a tribe known as the Quechua, who have their own special customs and special language. In the picture she is shown with a llama, an animal found commonly in Peru. The country is located on the continent of South America.

The great Inca civilization built their capital at Cuzco. Nearby a river runs through the Urubamba Valley, also known as the "Sacred Valley."

One of the most important places in Peru is the city of Machu Picchu built over 600 years ago. It was built high atop a mountain at an elevation of 8,000 feet. It was so high that it was called "the city in the clouds". The skilled builders were the ancient Inca people. The city was so well hidden that, during a war with Spain, the enemy never even knew of its existence, and therefore never tried to conquer it. Over time, the city was forgotten and lost to the world. No one knows why the people who lived there left only a hundred years after it was built.

For 500 years, the beautiful stone city sat atop the mountain in silence. It was completely unknown to the world until an American explorer named Hiram Bingham discovered it in 1911. He was amazed to see how perfectly the city had been built, with rocks cut so well that they fit together perfectly without having mortar between them. There were hundreds of stone terraces to grow food, and even an observatory to study the stars.

# United States

This boy from the United States is like many other young American boys. He belongs to a little league team, loves to play outdoors and enjoys going to football games with his father.

When school is not in session, he likes to go on trips with his parents. One year they went to Niagara Falls. Niagara Falls has three main waterfalls on the border between Canada and the United States. These are the Horseshoe Falls, the American Falls and the Bridal Veil Falls. People come from all over the world to see this beautiful place. Sometimes the mist is carried upwards on the wind and it feels like a light rain. Visitors can even take a boat ride underneath the falls, and wear a raincoat to keep dry.

Other vacation places to see in the United States are the national parks. One of the most famous is Yellowstone National Park in Wyoming, where there are spectacular geysers, and amazing wild animals roaming freely.

When the Europeans came to this land, the newcomers did not understand the ways of the Indians, and tried to change them. Today, people realize that it is often our cultural differences and traditions which make us stronger as individuals and enrich us as a nation.

The statue of a famous Indian called the "Crazy Horse Monument" in South Dakota is carved out of a mountain, and is 563 feet high. The head alone is 87 feet high. When it is finished, it will be the largest statue in the world.

# Cambodia

The young girl in the picture lives in a wooden house with her family in a small village in Cambodia. She often helps her mother take care of her younger brothers and sisters. The family practices the Buddhist religion, and there is a small shrine in their home where the family prays.

The Kingdom of Cambodia is also called "Kampuchea". Cambodia is located in Southeast Asia. Twelve centuries ago, the first king, Jayavarman, founded the Khmer Empire.

The largest religious complex in the world is located in a place called Angkor Wat. Some of the most beautiful temples, unlike any others in the world, are located here. These include the Temple of Bayon with it spacious stone courtyard, the mysterious citadel of Angkor Thom, and the shrine of Banteay Srei. The temples at Angkor Wat were originally Hindu places of worship. Their construction and design were largely influenced by monks and worshippers from India. Gradually, however, they became Buddhist shrines.

Today the jungles have encroached upon the ancient sites, with large tree roots and vines winding themselves around the old stones and temples. In the 1970's, during long and bitter clashes with the communist-led Khmer Rouge, many people died. Today, there are 15 million people living in Cambodia. Farming and tourism are two of the major industries. Today Cambodia is ruled by the Cambodia Peoples' Party and a Prime Minister.

# Ireland

This young Irish girl lives in a village called West Town on Tory Island, off the coast of Donegal in Ireland. Her family raises chickens on their small farm. Some evenings her family will sing together, and her uncle will play his accordion. Music and dance have always been important to the Irish culture.

It can be very stormy here because of the powerful waters of the North Atlantic Ocean. It is a friendly place where everyone knows everyone on the small island, and they sometimes meet for coffee or stop for a chat in the street.

Ireland is a large island west of Great Britain in the North Atlantic. It is the third largest island in Europe, and is often called the "Emerald Isle" because of its rich green landscape, rolling hills and forests. The shamrock is an emblem of Ireland dating to St. Patrick, who had been born in England, but was captured and taken to Ireland as a teenager by slave traders. He escaped, but later returned, and for forty years preached, and won the hearts of the people.

Ireland is part of the United Kingdom. It is divided into the Republic of Ireland in the south, and Northern Ireland. There is archaeological evidence that people have lived in this region for 12,000 years. Today over 5 million people live here.

At beautiful Blarney Castle, the tradition of kissing the Blarney Stone is said to grant a person the "gift of persuasion".

# Damaraland

The young men in the photo are wearing the traditional clothes of the Damara tribe, which include animal skins, and in particular leopard skin. While they may sometimes wear modern clothing, their tribal clothes are worn to special events and celebrations.

Damaraland is a remote region in southwest Africa which is now part of Namibia. It lies between the Kalahari Desert to the east and the Namib Desert to the west. The lofty Brandberg Mountain rises in the distance. The climate is very dry here, and some years there is no rain at all. The massive sand dunes have the rich red color typical of the Kalihari Desert.

Nearby is an area called Twyfelfontein. In this area, large imposing rock outcroppings rise from the desert floor. Here among these gorges and ravines are "petroglyphs", which include about 5,000 stone images etched into the rocks with primitive tools, and also a smaller number of paintings. They were left here 6,000 years ago. Some scientists believe that the original San tribe, who are believed to have produced these drawings, were the earliest people to inhabit the earth.

These rock images depict ancient hunters who once inhabited this region. The most famous image is called the "White Lady of the Brandberg", discovered by a German surveyor in 1917. It depicts a woman leading female hunters who have just captured an antelope. Nearby is a petrified forest with enormous fallen trees hardened like rock over the centuries.

# China

This young girl is enjoying summer near her family home in a rural village. She and her brother enjoy riding in the wooden cart pulled by the family's oxen when her parents go to work in the rice paddies.

China is one of the oldest countries in the world dating back 3,000 years to the Shang Dynasty, but prehistoric pottery and arrowheads have been found dating back over 10,000 years. Today there are over 1.4 billion people in China.

In the city of Beijing, the capital of China, there is a gated palace called "The Forbidden City". It was once home only to the Chinese Emperor, his family, and those who served him. The palace complex has over 8,000 rooms. Nearby, there is also a wide public plaza called Tiananmen Square. It is the largest public square in the world.

An amazing discovery was made in 1974 near a small town called Xian, when local farmers were building a well. They found partly exposed statues buried near the tomb of the first Chinese Emperor Qin Shi who died about 2,200 years ago. Altogether there were 8,000 life-size statues of soldiers and horsemen. They were in standing poses, as if they were ready to protect the Emperor. There were also hundreds of full-size statues of horses.

For centuries, poets have written about the majestic beauty of China's Yangtze River winding through deep rock gorges and forested cliffs.

# Madagascar

The young girl in the picture lives with her family in south central Madagascar. She helps her parents on their small farm and lives very far from the nearest city.

Madagascar is one of the most interesting placed on earth. Years ago it was part of the continent of Africa. Due to the breakup of the land masses and continental drift, the island broke away. It is now in the Indian Ocean, about 250 miles east of the southern coast of Africa.

For over 80 million years it developed in isolation. Three-fourths of all the animals and plants in Madagascar are found nowhere else on earth. One of these is the lemur, a small jungle animal which lives primarily in trees. Some lemurs can jump 30 feet from one tree to the other. There are several varieties of lemurs only found on this island, except for those who have been taken to zoos in other parts of the world.

Once, the entire island was covered with ancient forests. People, who came here two thousand years ago, cut down trees for their homes and buildings, and now most of the dense, beautiful forests are gone. This endangers both the lemurs and the other wild animals who had safely lived here millions of years before humans arrived on the island.

There are now 18 different tribes living in Madagascar. Small towns usually have a "village elder". This man is responsible for the welfare and safety of his village.

# Kenya

The young girl in the picture belongs to the Samburu tribe in Africa. The people in this tribe are sometimes "semi-nomadic", which means that they will often move from place to place to find new grazing land for their cattle. They will leave their old homes and carry all their belongings to the new place tied to the backs of camels. Camels are very valuable to the tribe. The people depend on camels for milk, clothing, trade and transportation. It is the custom for the groom to give a gift of eight camels to the family of the woman he wishes to marry.

The name "Kenya" comes from a Kikuyu word meaning "God's Resting Place." The country is located on the coast of the Indian Ocean. Today Kenya has 45 million people. It became independent from England in 1963, and one year later became the Republic of Kenya. The capital at Nairobi is Africa's main launching point for safari adventures. Nearby is Kenya's world-famous Masai Mara, which covers over 600 square miles, and has one of Africa's greatest concentrations of wild and exotic animals. Kenya is also famous for its exports of coffee and tea.

Just across the border at Olduvai Gorge, important archaeological work on man's primitive ancestors was carried out by researchers Mary and Louis Leakey. In 1984, new researchers at Kenya's Lake Turkana, found a full skeleton called "Turkana Boy", dating back 1.6 million years. There is evidence that human-like primates lived here as early as 20 million years ago.

# Japan

The young girl in the picture is at the Children's Festival at the Meiji Shrine in Tokyo, Japan. The country is a unique mixture of the old and the new, and Tokyo is one of its most interesting cities. Here are Buddhist temples and ancient gardens, blending with the modern day world of streamlined bullet trains traveling at great speeds past soaring skyscrapers.

Most of Japan is built on four islands: Hokkaido, Kyushu, Shikoka and Honshu. Tokyo, the modern capital and largest city on Honshu Island, has nearly 9 million people, and including its outlying suburbs has a total population of nearly 14 million.

The cherry blossom is a national emblem of Japan. Its serene colors often frame Mount Fuji, Japan's highest mountain and one of the country's most stunning views. Beautiful Kyoto has Buddhist temples, imperial gardens and lavish palaces. It also has hundreds of brilliant red columns which serve as gates for the Inari Shinto Shrine built in the eighth century.

The legendary land of intricately woven silk kimonos and elaborate tea celebrations retains the traditional ceremonies for new generations. But one of the most important places in Japan is the World Peace Museum at Hiroshima. This museum, which explores past world conflicts, now urges all nations to choose cooperation as a solution for resolving world issues in the future. It is a plea for world peace.

# Burma

The young boy in the picture is a monk in the town of Bagan in the region of Mandalay. Burma is known as a place of ancient temples and pagodas built almost a thousand years ago. It is located in Southeast Asia.

This young man was only ten years old, when he began his studies to become a monk. He is taught to read the ancient scriptures of his people, and says prayers at many times throughout the day. In this small area in which he lives, over 4,000 Buddhist temples were built in the eleventh century.

The country of Burma, located west of China and Thailand, was closed to outsiders for many years. It was considered mysterious and unexplored. Today, it is called Myanmar, and is open to visitors. The population of the country is currently over 51 million people.

This is a mountainous country with ancient forests. Mountain streams from the Himalayan Mountains fill its largest river called the Irrawaddy. Along this winding river, life goes on as it has for centuries. At Inle Lake, the Intha Tribe builds homes on high stilts over the water. Because Burma is in a monsoon region, some areas receive over 200 inches of rain each year. In the jungle areas there are rhinoceros, elephants and wild buffalo.

The Shwedagon Paya Pagoda overlooks Rangoon. Its golden exterior has precious jewels, including 5,000 diamonds, embedded at the top. It is believed to be about 2,000 years old.

# Canada

Most of the people in Canada live in cities and towns very similar to those in America. A small number of Canadians, however, inhabit a very unique place in the northernmost part of Canada. It is called Nunavut, and is one of three official territories belonging to Canada. The other two territories are the Northwest Territories and the Yukon. Wildlife such as caribou, polar bears and walruses abound in this rugged environment.

The young boy in the picture lives near Grise Fjord on Ellsmere Island at Nunavut. This region is isolated and very cold during most of the year. It is also a beautiful place of rugged mountains, ice and deep blue water. The small communities of people have learned to survive and flourish in the challenging environment. They have kept alive the skills and customs of their ancestors in this remarkable place they call home.

The name "Nunavut" in the native tribal language means "our land". The young boy in the picture belongs to the Inuit tribe. They live much as their ancestors lived here for hundreds of years. They wear similar traditional clothing made of furs and animal skins. Their families build igloos of snow bricks, and travel by dogsled and kayak. There are only 32,000 people in Nunavut. This region has been inhabited continuously for 4,000 years by the indigenous, native people. Their first contact with the outside world occurred in the 1500's, when the English explorer, Martin Frobisher, attempted to find a Northwest Passage connecting the Pacific and Atlantic Oceans.

# India

The young girl in the picture enjoys wearing the traditional Indian clothing of her people. She lives in a city near Delhi, and enjoys going to school with her friends.

India is a republic in South Asia. It has the second largest population of any country in the world, after China. The history of India goes back 5,000 years. It is a land of contrasts, from the soaring Himalaya Mountains to the country's broad coastlines on the Indian Ocean, the Bay of Bengal and the Arabian Sea.

India has been the birthplace of two major religions. One of these is the Hindu religion founded about 2000 BC, and believed to be the oldest religion in the world. Another major religion, Buddhism, originated here in the fifth century BC.

No landmark in India can compare to the Taj Mahal. Built in 1631 by Shah Jahan, it was a monument expressing his love for his wife, Mumtaz, who had died giving birth to their fourteenth child. During the last eight years of his life, Shah Jahan was imprisoned by his own son, who had seized power. From his prison in the royal residence at Agra, he spent the last years of his life gazing upon the Taj Mahal.

Through the British East India Company, England had control of India from the 1800's. India did not become independent until 1947. The Ganges River in India is considered to be a sacred river, and pilgrims from all over the world come to bathe in its water.

# Namibia

This young girl is shown at her school in southern Namibia near the city of Windhoek, Namibia. She belongs to the Herero Tribe.

However, many people in her tribe still live outside the cities and practice a nomadic lifestyle. In those cases, the women collect firewood, cook and do handicrafts. They also carry water to their villages and take care of the goats and cows.

Namibia became independent in 1991. The long expanse of coastline in western Namibia is called the Skeleton Coast. It is a land of massive sand dunes and natural beauty. Along that coast hundreds of flamingos gather in the blue water of the Atlantic, and large seal populations live along the shore. Also here are the remains of many shipwrecks going back hundreds of years. There have been dangerous ocean storms here since the earliest times.

Inland in Namibia, particularly in the north near the Etosha Game Park, safaris for elephants, rhinoceros and lions bring visitors from all over the world. Fortunately, tourists are restricted to photographing them, but not harming them.

Only 20 years ago in Namibia, the numbers of animals had been drastically reduced due to poaching, or illegal hunting parties who killed endangered species. Today world conservation efforts have replenished the number of animals, and especially the lion population in parts of Namibia. Herds of giraffe, zebra and black rhinos are now often seen crossing this magnificent landscape.

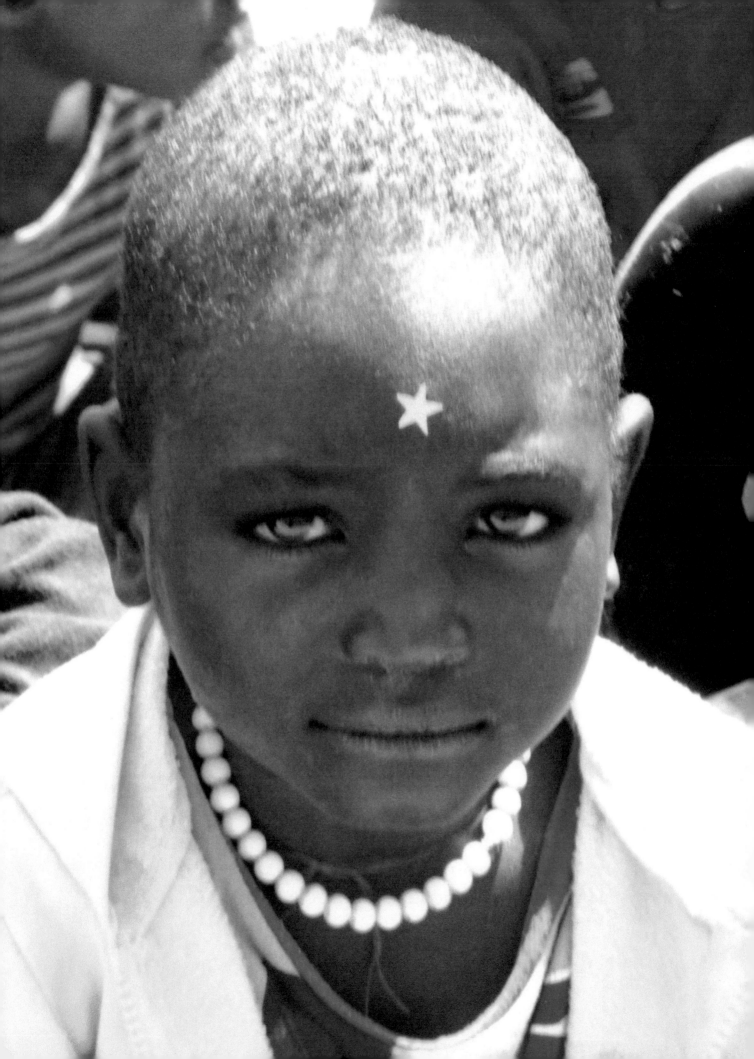

# Mongolia

This young Kazakh girl is competing in the Golden Eagle Festival in Altai, Mongolia. The festival demonstrates hunting skills using a trained eagle. The event takes place each October in western Mongolia. This art is a tradition which has been practiced in Mongolia for 4,000 years. Horse racing and archery competitions also take place at this festival. A traditional contest called the "Bushkashi", involves a tug-of-war between two horseback riders using a traditional goatskin.

The vast country of Mongolia is one of the most remote regions in the world. Located north of China and South of Russia, it is the land of the famous Gobi Desert. Eighty million years ago dinosaurs lived here in an area known as the Red Cliffs. The rare snow leopard also lives here.

Today the vast territory is traveled by nomad herders. Their round homes, called gers, have a wooden frame, and are made of sheep wool, felt and a waterproof covering. When these people move to find new grazing land, these homes are taken apart and carried to the new place, where they are reassembled.

On the wide vistas, cows, sheep, goats and horses often wander freely. In the morning the herdsmen gather their own animals. In the cold and harsh climate, adapting to this life can be challenging. One of their most indispensable animals is the yak. These animals provide milk, meat, hides and transportation. Their long hair is also used to make blankets and clothes.

# Viet Nam

Vietnam is a South Asian country which faces the South China Sea. For over a thousand years from the first to the mid-ninth century, Vietnam was part of Imperial China. However, this region was also inhabited much earlier. Skeletons of **Homo erectus**, a form of early primitive man, were found in caves in North Vietnam. These were dated by archeologists to 500,000 BC.

Today Vietnam has a population of 90 million people. The area is known for its sandy beaches. One of its most beautiful places is Halong Bay, where towering limestone cliffs rise steeply out of the water. Some of these rocky outcroppings are fringed with dense green forests.

Halong Bay is called the "Bay of the Descending Dragon". Ancient myths say that the dragons came down from heaven, and out of their mouths jade and precious gems fell into the bay. These gems then became the exotic and beautiful islands which now spread over the deep pristine blue water of the bay. There are over 1,600 of these islands in Halong Bay. Fishing villages and floating houses rest in the deep blue water. Artists have painted this spectacular scenery for centuries.

Although Vietnamese is the official language, French is also widely spoken. Today, the law also requires that English is taught in the schools.